What Families Are For

Fabiola Sepulveda

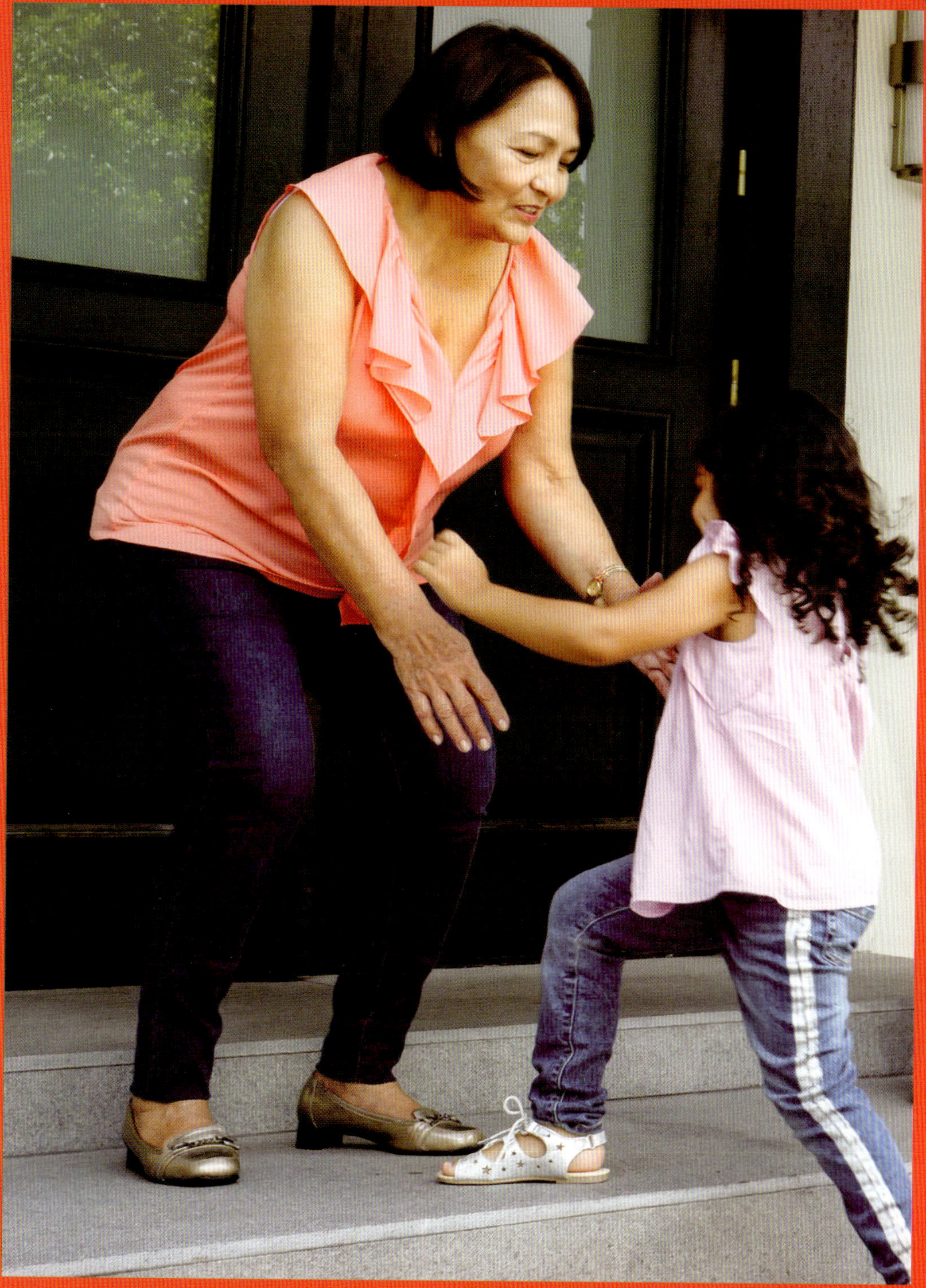

Notes for the Grown-ups

This wordless book allows for a rich shared reading experience for children who do not yet know how to read words or who are beginning to learn. Children can look at the pages to gather information from what they see, and they can suggest text to tell the story.

To extend this reading experience, do one or more of the following:

Discuss what makes a family a family.

Introduce vocabulary such as these words when looking at the pictures and telling the story you see:

- comfort
- cuddles
- exercise
- food
- health
- helping
- home
- learning
- love
- play
- safety
- shelter
- teaching
- togetherness

Talk about additional things families do and more ways they play a role in the child's life. Every family is unique, and the things families do are limitless.

After reading the pictures, come back to the book again and again. Rereading is an excellent tool for building literacy skills.

Encourage the child to make a family book of their own with photos or drawings they take or make.

Consultant

Cynthia Malo, M.A.Ed.

Publishing Credits

Rachelle Cracchiolo, M.S.Ed., *Publisher*
Emily R. Smith, M.A.Ed., *SVP of Content Development*
Véronique Bos, *VP of Creative*
Dona Herweck Rice, *Senior Content Manager*

Image Credits: all images from iStock and/or Shutterstock

Library of Congress Cataloging-in-Publication Data
Names: Sepulveda, Fabiola, author.
Title: What families are for / Fabiola Sepulveda.
Description: Huntington Beach : Teacher Created Materials, Inc, [2024] |
 Audience: Ages 3-9 | Summary: "Families offer so many things, from
 providing safety to giving love. Look at some of the wonderful things
 that families do"-- Provided by publisher.
Identifiers: LCCN 2024007615 (print) | LCCN 2024007616 (ebook) | ISBN
 9798765961216 (paperback) | ISBN 9798765967430 (ebook)
Subjects: LCSH: Families--Juvenile literature.
Classification: LCC HQ744 .S387 2024 (print) | LCC HQ744 (ebook) | DDC
 306.85--dc23/eng/20240215
LC record available at https://lccn.loc.gov/2024007615
LC ebook record available at https://lccn.loc.gov/2024007616

TCM Teacher
Created
Materials

5482 Argosy Avenue
Huntington Beach, CA 92649
www.tcmpub.com
ISBN 979-8-7659-6121-6
© 2025 Teacher Created Materials, Inc.
Printed by: 926. Printed in: Malaysia. PO#: PO11723